Real Size Science

Animals

Rebecca Rissman

Raintree is an imprint of Capstone Global Library Limited, a company incorporated in England and Wales having its registered office at 7 Pilgrim Street, London, EC4V 6LB – Registered company number: 6695582

www.raintreepublishers.co.uk
myorders@raintreepublishers.co.uk

Edited by Rebecca Rissman, Daniel Nunn, and John-Paul Wilkins
Designed by Joanna Malivoire and Tim Bond
Picture research by Ruth Blair
Production by Sophia Argyris
Originated by Capstone Global Library Ltd
Printed and bound in China by South China Printing Company

ISBN 978 1 406 26349 7
17 16 15 14 13
10 9 8 7 6 5 4 3 2 1

British Library Cataloguing in Publication Data
Rissman, Rebecca.
Animals. – (Real size science)
591.4'1-dc23
A full catalogue record for this book is available from the British Library.

Acknowledgements
We would like to thank the following for permission to reproduce photographs: Shutterstock pp. 4, 7, 8 (© Eric Isselee), 5 (© Potapov Alexander, © stock09, © tristan tan, © Alberto Masnovo), 6 (© risteski goce), 9 main(© Anastasija Popova), 9 inset (© Four Oaks), 10 (© Tyler Fox), 11 main (© Fernando Cortes), 11 inset (© Ekaterina Pokrovsky), 12 (© Dima Fadeev), 13 (© Glovatskiy), 14 (© Steve Byland), 15 main (© FRabanedo), 15 inset (© Johan Swanepoel), 16 (© randon Alms), 17 (© Dirk Ercken), 18 (© Tischenko Irina), 19 (© Rui Manuel Teles Gomes), 20 (© stockpix4u), 21 (© Kletr), 22 main, 22 inset (© clearviewstock), 23 gills (© DmZ), 23 scales (© Nataliia Melnychuk).

Cover photograph of a male American bullfrog (*Lithobates catesbeianus*) reproduced with permission of Shutterstock (© Ilias Strachinis).

We would like to thank Dee Reid and Nancy Harris for their invaluable help in the preparation of this book.

Every effort has been made to contact copyright holders of material reproduced in this book. Any omissions will be rectified in subsequent printings if notice is given to the publisher.

Disclaimer

Contents

Animal sizes

Animals are different sizes.

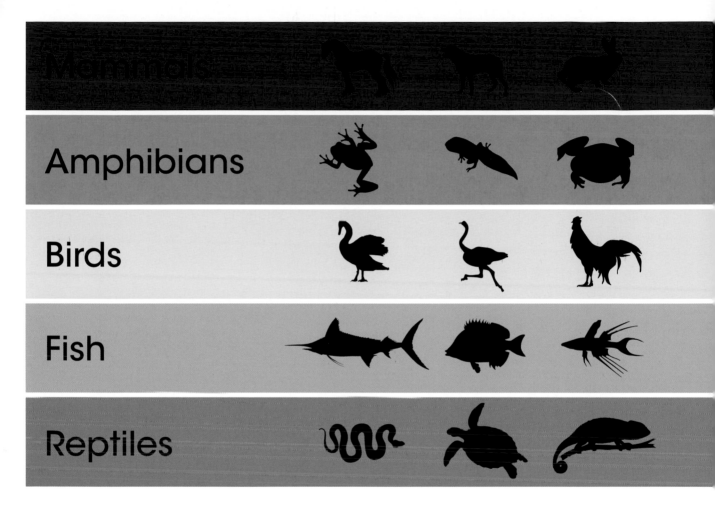

Mammals

Amphibians

Birds

Fish

Reptiles

Animals are organized into groups.

Mammals

Mammals drink milk when they are babies.

Real Size

Most mammals are
covered with hair.

A dormouse is a small mammal.

Real size

hoof

Real size

A horse is a large mammal.

It has four hard hooves to walk on.

Amphibians

Amphibians live on land and water.

They lay many eggs.

Real size

Real Size

A cane toad is a large amphibian.
Its skin can be poisonous!

Birds

Birds have feathers and wings.

feathers

wings

Birds hatch from eggs.

A hummingbird is a small bird.

Real Size

beak

An ostrich is a large bird.
It uses its beak to eat
grasses and seeds.

Real size

Fish

Fish live in water.

Fish have scales and fins.

fin

egg →

Fish lay soft eggs.

A clownfish is a small fish.

Real size

gills →

A trout is a large fish.

Fishes' gills help them to breathe.

Reptiles

Reptiles have scales.

Most reptiles hatch from eggs.

An alligator is a large reptile.

This is the size of one of its eyes.

Real size surprise!

This is the smallest frog on Earth.
You could hold it on your finger!

Real Siz

Picture glossary

 **beak** hard, pointed mouth that birds have

 **feathers** body covering on birds. Feathers help birds to fly.

 **gills** parts of a fish's body that help it to breathe

 **scales** small, thin plates that cover fish and reptiles

Index

Notes for parents and teachers

Before reading
- Engage children in a discussion about animal sizes. Ask children to think of different ways we describe size, such as tall, short, wide, or thin.
- Tell children that we can use tools, such as rulers, to measure size. We can also use body parts, such as hand lengths and foot lengths, to measure size.

After reading
- Write clownfish, cane toad, hummingbird, and horse on the board. Ask children to put them in order according to their size.
- Ask children to turn to page 8. Using a ruler, how tall is the dormouse?
- Ask children to turn to page 9. Using their hands as measurement tools, how wide is the horse's hoof (e.g., one palm width, or one and a half palm widths)?

24